Also by Charles Roth

Mind: The Master Power

A Twelve-Power Meditation Exercise

Charles Roth

unity®
Books

Unity Village, MO 64065-0001

Second Edition, seventh printing 2011

To place an order, call the Customer Service
Department: 1-800-669-0282, or visit us
online at *www.unity.org.*

Cover design: Karen Rizzo

CONTENTS

Charles Fillmore's book, *The Twelve Powers of Man*, was written in 1930, and since that time has been taught time and again in Unity classes.

However, the emphasis has usually been on the theory, the intellectually exciting lectures about the various faculties and body centers.

If the theory is valid and good, it would seem that putting it into practice is the logical follow-through. The purpose of these lessons is to help you focus on the various body centers and, through the power of the word, to quicken the faculties and hasten the process of regeneration of your physical body.

Although each lesson contains a meditation on the faculty discussed in the lesson, the last lesson contains the complete Twelve-Power Meditation Exercise.

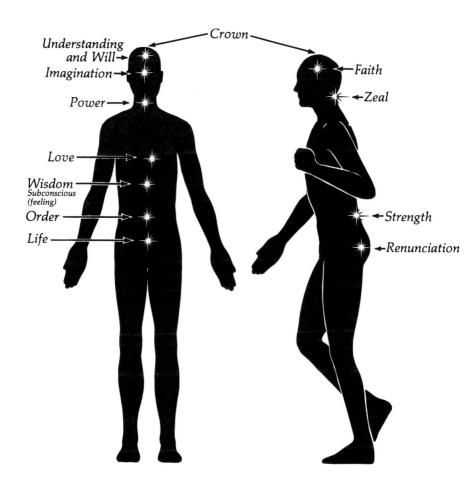

FAITH

Peter—Pineal Gland

Charles Fillmore was the co-founder of Unity School of Christianity, and in my opinion, a genius in the realm of spiritual thought and teaching.

He wrote *The Twelve Powers of Man* in 1930, and since then there have been numerous printings of it. It is not an easy book to read or to understand. It is not the typical inspirational book that assures us over and over to "let go and let God," or to "hang in there with faith."

Neither is it a textbook for beginners in which basic spiritual principles are introduced.

1

A Twelve-Power Meditation Exercise

There is a need for inspirational books, and a need for textbooks on spiritual principles; but there also is a place for stronger spiritual substance. Fillmore's *The Twelve Powers of Man* addresses itself to those who are acquainted with the basics but hunger and thirst for greater understanding.

The twelve powers refer to twelve faculties of mind. These faculties of mind are symbolized in the Old Testament by the twelve tribes of Israel, and in the New Testament by the twelve disciples.

Charles Fillmore goes one step farther. He suggests that each of the twelve faculties has a "center" in a specific area of the physical body.

The object of this group of lessons is to familiarize you with the function, character, and location of these disciple-faculties; and then, in meditation, to quicken them spiritually so that they may more capably serve the spiritual self of your indwelling Christ.

Just as Jesus needed, and therefore called and trained, His twelve disciples, so do you (the I AM of you) call or awaken and train your disciple-faculties of mind in order to aid you in lifting your spiritual self out of bondage to the outer world of effects that has you enslaved and entranced.

The format of these lessons is to discuss a

specific disciple-faculty and its location in the physical body, and then to suggest a meditation to quicken and spiritualize that faculty.

In this lesson we will work with the first and primary faculty of mind: *faith*.

The faith faculty is symbolized by the disciple Peter. Peter, you will recall, was the first disciple to be called by Jesus. And it was Peter to whom Jesus said: "On this rock I will build my church" (Mt. 16:18).

Today the word *church*, as used in this passage of the Bible, was originally *ecclesia*, a word that means, "called out ones." There are many different denominations, many different interpretations of Jesus' teachings, but there is only one "church of Jesus"; it is an invisible church, composed of persons of any denomination, or of none who, like Peter, recognize the Christ in Jesus and realize that the same Christ indwells all persons. As Paul wrote, "The mystery hidden for ages and generations but now made manifest . . . . Christ in you, the hope of glory" (Col. 1:26, 27).

Your disciple-faculty of faith, Peter, is the first to be called to be quickened. But wait just a moment—when Jesus first met him, Peter's name wasn't Peter, it was Simon. The name *Simon* means "hearing, understanding,

obeying." Jesus changed Simon's name to Peter
at that moment when Simon, henceforth to be
known as Peter, exclaimed, "You are the
Christ" (Mk. 8:29).

In short, as you listen (Simon) and are
receptive to the spiritual dimension of life, as
you begin to understand and to obey your
inner thoughts instead of the opinions of others
that you have previously accepted as yours,
there comes a point when faith supplants your
indecision and searching. Simon becomes Peter,
and upon this faith in your indwelling Christ
you proceed to build or live your life.

However, to be realistic, there come times
when your faith wavers, vacillates. Some
unexpected event occurs that overwhelms you
and makes you feel helpless, or some
responsibility is thrust on you that seems as
impossible of successful handling as moving a
mountain. It flattens your faith like a
punctured balloon. The Bible predicted such
times.

Remember how Peter (faith) vacillated and
even denied knowing Jesus? Peter tried to
walk on water, but suddenly he began to doubt
and started to sink.

We, too, at times get ourselves into
precarious positions, and suddenly the roof
falls in, and our faith in God reverses into a

belief that the outer appearance is mightier than the indwelling spirit of God. Fear is faith in reverse—faith in the power of the outer condition, instead of faith in the power of the inner Christ.

Jesus, who represents the spiritual I AM in us, reached out His hand to Peter. The winds ceased, Peter was shaken loose from his hypnotic entrancement to the seeming threatening power of the outer condition, and all was well.

So it is with you and me. We often find some experience too much for our developing faith. Doubts and fears crowd in, and we feel ourselves sinking into hopeless, human helplessness.

This is the time to mentally and spiritually reach out for the hand of Christ through your spiritual identity, your sense of I AM.

You do this by the power of the word, by speaking the word of faith into the farthest corridors of your mind. Affirm:

*I AM strong in my faith. I AM
being lifted out of fear and
doubt. I AM secure in the
protective love and power of God!*

Yes, faith is the number one faculty of mind, just as Peter was the first disciple whom Jesus called into God's service.

A Twelve-Power Meditation Exercise

Faith moves mountains, or what appear to
be mountains to those who feel they are alone,
helpless, with only their information-holding
intellect as a defense against a seemingly cold,
cruel outer world.

We are talking about faith in God, not faith
in yourself, or faith in your position or prestige
or your carefully accumulated stock portfolio.
Faith in anything less than the creative and
sustaining cause back of all that appears has an
inherent flaw in it that is bound to give way
sometime, someplace.

It is indeed like a building on sand, which is
sound when things are going all right, but
which quickly washes away when an unlooked-
for flood comes sweeping down!

You develop or spiritualize your faculty of
faith through meditation. Yes, it is also
developed through meeting experiences with
faith; but that part is more the "testing" of it
than the developing of it.

Now we come to the meditation technique
for quickening your faculty of faith, for
awakening your faculty of faith to its designed
office or purpose—faith in God!

Charles Fillmore, in *The Twelve Powers of
Man*, located the physical center for the faith-
faculty in the pineal gland, which is located in
the middle of the head.

Begin your Twelve-Power Meditation by sitting quietly for a moment until you feel relaxed. Then focus your attention on the crown of the head (which represents the Christ center) and think a thought similar to this:

The Christ of God is quickened in me!

Next, move your center of attention to your forehead, often thought of as representing the conscious level of mind. Realize that you are consciously aware that the Christ of God is being quickened in you. Say or think:

I AM aware that the Christ
of God is quickened in me.

Now move your center of attention to the solar plexus, which represents the subconscious level of mind. In order to accept your awareness that the Christ of God is being quickened in you at the deepest level of your being, affirm:

I AM grateful that the Christ of
God is being quickened in me.

Gratitude is an emotion, and the subconscious is the seat of your feelings, your emotions.

Now let your center of attention travel to the middle of the head, the faith center, and softly affirm:

The Christ in me calls forth Peter,
my disciple-faculty of faith.

A Twelve-Power Meditation Exercise

As you do this, visualize Jesus speaking the words, "According to your faith be it done unto you." After a time conclude by saying:
I AM grateful!
The color key for faith is deep blue. Let the color blue, when you see it in the late afternoon sky, or wear a blue item of clothing, remind you of faith—true blue faith in God!

STRENGTH

Andrew—Small of Back

Cora Fillmore, in her book, *Christ Enthroned in Man*, states:

"Nothing so uplifts, nothing so frees from care and worry, nothing so brings the thought of victory as being established in that sustaining strength which cannot know weakness."

The disciple who represents the faculty of *strength* is Andrew.

The name *Andrew* is from the Greek, and literally means "strong, a strong man, manly."

Andrew is the brother of Peter. When, in the Twelve-Power Meditation, you reunite these brothers, *faith* (Peter) and *strength* (Andrew), you have a spiritual team that will carry you through the most adverse circumstances.

As we mentioned in the first lesson, Charles Fillmore not only draws a correspondence between each of the disciples and the twelve faculties or powers of mind, he also designates a certain area of the physical body as the ruling "center" of each faculty.

We learned that the faith faculty, represented by Peter, has its physical center in the pineal gland, located in the middle of the head.

The strength faculty is located in the part of the side and back between the ribs and the pelvis. It is also called the "loins."

It is a part of folk wisdom to associate the small of the back, or loins, with strength. To "gird one's loins" is an archaic phrase used when one was going out to meet a challenge that required physical strength or stamina.

In infantry basic training we often used the phrase, "Oh, my achin' back!" when we were physically exhausted. It is significant, and to me exciting, to find the many associations between concepts of strength or lack of strength, and the small of the back or loins which Charles Fillmore describes as the strength center.

One of the largest muscles of the body is

located at this strength center. It is called the Sacrospinalis muscle. It has nine divisions, with the last division inserting into the neck and head. In short, there is a direct physical connection between the strength center in the small of the back (Andrew) and the faith center in the head (Peter).

Just one more bit of significant information my research revealed: A triangular bone called the sacrum is located at this physical center. The dictionary reports that the word *sacrum* is derived from the Latin, and means "sacred bone." Apparently this strength area of the body had special significance in ancient religious ritual.

Let's talk a little bit about the idea of strength.

First there is physical strength. As you, in meditation, send your word of Truth to the strength center at the small of the back, you find weakness draining away; you are actually strengthened in a physical sense. I say this out of experience, for I use this Twelve-Power Meditation each morning.

Then there is strength in a mental sense. You will find through meditating on this center that you are better able to think for yourself. You are not easily swayed by the opinions and manipulative techniques of others. You have the courage, confidence, and strength to stand by your own opinions and convictions.

Strength on an emotional level expresses as the ability to remain calm in the face of outer temptations to get upset or angry, or to "go to pieces." When a series of difficult experiences hits you, each drains a bit of emotional energy from you. When your emotional energy level is low, some little thing may cause you to break into tears, or "go to pieces." As you send the word of Truth into your strength center, you find your emotional energy well able to handle the inevitable "bumps" of life.

You may wonder what I mean by "send the word of Truth" to your faith center in the head, and the strength center in the loins or small of the back. This is a vital part of the Twelve-Power Meditation technique.

Most methods or techniques of meditation do not involve nor are they concerned with the physical body. Oh, you begin all meditation by relaxing and in one way or another blessing the body. But then you usually say, in effect, "Okay, body, now rest and wait while I do the real meditating on the mental and spiritual planes."

The genius of Charles Fillmore shows through in his original and unique concept of bringing the physical body into the actual meditation experience! Meditation involves the whole person: Spirit, mind, and body.

You send the word of Truth by invisible currents of energy. This was demonstrated by Jesus when He sent His Word and healed the centurion's servant. The spiritual mechanics are very simple, although as in all things, you improve with practice.

In sending your word of Truth to the various faculty or disciple-centers in your body, place the focus of your attention on that area of your body. Then, as you speak or think words such as *Christ in me quickens the disciple-faculty of strength* with your focus of attention in the strength area, spiritual energy, Christ energy, flows on invisible currents to that center!

It is time to incorporate this second disciple-faculty into the actual practice of the Twelve-Power Meditation technique.

Remember, Jesus and His twelve disciples metaphysically symbolize or represent the Christ in you and the twelve faculties or powers through which the Christ expresses.

Begin your meditation by sitting quietly for a moment until you feel relaxed. Then focus your attention at the very crown of the head (which represents the Christ center) and think a thought similar to this:

*The Christ of God is
quickened in me!*

Next, move your center of attention to your
forehead, which you think of as representing
your conscious level of mind. To realize that
you are consciously aware that the Christ of
God is being quickened in you, say or think:

*I am aware that the Christ of God
is quickened in me.*

Now move your attention to the solar
plexus, which represents the subconscious level
of mind, and in order to accept your awareness
that the Christ of God is being quickened in
you at the deepest level of your being, affirm:

*I am grateful that the Christ of
God is being quickened in me.*

Now let your center of attention travel to the
middle of the head, the faith center, and softly
affirm:

*The Christ in me calls forth Peter,
my disciple-faculty of faith.*

Next, focus your attention through your
body to the small of your back, the part of
your side and back between the lower ribs and
the pelvis. Softly speak the words of Truth:

*The Christ in me calls forth
Andrew, my disciple-faculty
of strength.*

I sometimes add:

*I AM "strong in the Lord and in the
strength of his might"* (Eph. 6:10).
After a time conclude by saying with feeling:
I AM grateful!
The color key for strength is light green, the
inspiring color of the spring leaves of trees as
new life and strength rise up from the roots.

WISDOM

James—Solar Plexus

Before we delve into the third disciple-faculty, let's go over the foundation principle once more.

The premise of the Twelve-Power Meditation technique is:

1. Jesus metaphysically represents the Christ in you.

2. The twelve disciples of Jesus represent the twelve faculties or powers of mind in you, through which the Christ unfolds and expresses.

3. Each of the twelve disciple-faculties has a ganglionic center in the physical body.

It is this third part of the basic

premise that is unique to Unity and came through the genius of Charles Fillmore. I think you will agree that it appeals to the logic of the mind and to the heart.

We are threefold beings: Spirit, mind, and body. Or "I AM," "I think," and "I express." It seems natural and logical that each faculty is represented on all three planes: the spiritual, the mental, and the physical.

Faith, for instance, is a universal idea on the spiritual plane, a faculty of mind on the mental plane, and because Spirit, mind, and body are one unit, faith logically has a "center" in the physical body!

In the Twelve-Power Meditation Exercise, we first realize our oneness with God through Christ. Then we "let" the indwelling Christ call forth the individual disciple-faculties; and as we do, we focus our attention on that part of the body over which each disciple-faculty presides.

We started with Peter, the first disciple called, who represents faith. The physical center is the pineal gland in the middle of the head.

Next came Andrew, who represents strength, and that center is in the loins, or small of the back.

Now we come to James, the son of Zebedee,

who represents the faculty, or mind-power, of wisdom, good judgment, and discrimination. The physical center for wisdom is the solar plexus. Let's turn to the dictionary to determine the location of the solar plexus.

"The large network of sympathetic nerves and ganglia located in the cavity behind the stomach and having branching tracts that supply the nerves to the abdominal viscera. Informally called the pit of the stomach."

Physiologically this center is very important, for it is in charge of the delicate chemical balance of the body. As Charles Fillmore wrote, "Every bit of food that we take into our stomachs must be intelligently and chemically treated at this center before it can be distributed to the many members waiting for this center's wise judgment to supply them with material to build bone, muscle, nerve, eye, ear, hair, nails—in fact every part of the organism."

What a job! No wonder it is the physical seat of wisdom, judgment, and discrimination between good and bad!

The solar plexus is also the seat of the subconscious level of mind. The body-wisdom of chemically treating and supplying the material to build and sustain the body is a subconscious function. In short, we do not consciously direct these processes.

The subconscious is also related to your "feeling" nature. All these tie together beautifully. For instance, when you hear distressing news, or a powerful thought of fear comes into your mind, you say, "Wow! I got a terrible sinking feeling in the pit of my stomach!"

When a son or daughter isn't eating as much as usual, you will say, "You are not eating. What is the matter? Are you in love?" Love, you see, is an emotion, and the excitement of love upsets the normal functioning of the digestive process in the solar plexus.

Or again, those who are continually emotionally excited with impatience, fear, ambition, or anger develop ulcers. These examples demonstrate the relationship between feelings or emotion and the wisdom center, the solar plexus, which is caused to malfunction because of the storms of emotion.

Have you ever had to make a decision, and when you made it said, "This feels right deep down in me"? By deep down didn't you mean in the solar plexus region?

Solomon metaphysically represents wisdom in the Bible. Sol means "sun"; Solomon means "the sun man." This same root is found in solar plexus. Sun, light, wisdom!

Solomon was a wise and great judge; he had

intuitive judgment. Remember when each of
two women claimed the same infant as her
natural child? Solomon commanded an
attendant to bring a sword and cut the child in
two, giving half to each woman. Of course, the
real mother begged him not to do this. She said
that she would give up the child first. Then
Solomon knew at once that she was the
mother. This is a clear example of wisdom.

The book of Proverbs was written by
Solomon, and as you read it you see how
many times and how highly he speaks of
wisdom.

"Happy is the man who finds wisdom, and
the man who gets understanding, for the gain
from it is better than gain from silver and its
profit better than gold" (Prov. 3:13-14).
Continuing to speak of wisdom, Solomon
writes, "She is more precious than jewels, and
nothing you desire can compare with her. Long
life is in her right hand; in her left hand are
riches and honor" (Prov. 3:15-16).

Another interesting biblical fact, dem-
onstrating the importance of the wisdom
faculty, is that many familiar Bible verses are
quoted as if God is speaking. On closer
examination, you will find that the Bible gives
"wisdom" as the speaker! For instance: "I love
those who love me, and those who seek me

diligently find me" (Prov. 8:17). God talking
about God? No. Wisdom is talking about
wisdom. "Riches and honor are with me,
enduring wealth and prosperity" (Prov. 8:18).
Or, "Endowing with wealth those who love
me, and filling their treasuries" (Prov. 8:21).

Wisdom is not information. Books,
universities, and libraries cannot give you
wisdom. Information, yes; but not wisdom and
good judgment. These can only arise from
within the individual.

Even life experience doesn't necessarily give
us wisdom. All older persons have had many
life experiences; and yet no one would claim
that all older persons are necessarily wise.
Many older persons are wise, of course; but
this is because they have learned to follow their
inner feelings instead of the textbook opinions
of others.

Solomon teaches us the first and primary
rule for obtaining wisdom. In 1 Kings 3:7,9, he
wrote, "And now, O Lord my God, thou hast
made thy servant king in place of David my
father, although I am but a little child; I do not
know how to go out or come in. . . . Give thy
servant therefore an understanding mind."

How closely this parallels Jesus' teaching that
we must become as little children!

In short, to obtain wisdom from within, we

must empty ourselves of previous pro-
gramming, previous beliefs and opinions.
Attain the inner attitude of "I don't know, and
I admit I don't know, but I am eager to learn."

Now let's work this wisdom-faculty into the
Twelve-Power Meditation Exercise.

As I stated in the previous lessons, begin by
placing your attention at the crown of your
head, representing the Christ center in you;
then lower it to your forehead, representing
your conscious level of mind, and then to your
solar plexus, representing the subconscious
level of mind.

At the crown of your head, affirm:
The Christ of God is quickened in me.

At your forehead, your conscious level of
awareness, affirm:
I AM aware that the Christ
of God is quickened in me.

Then, moving to the solar plexus region, the
seat of feeling, affirm:
I AM grateful that the Christ
of God is quickened in me.

Next, call forth Peter, your disciple-faculty
of faith, by letting your focus of attention
travel from the solar plexus to the faith center
in the middle of your head, and affirm
Christ in me calls forth Peter,
my disciple-faculty of faith.

I have mountain-moving
faith in God!

Now let your focus of attention drop to the small of your back, Andrew, the strength center, and affirm:

Christ in me calls forth Andrew,
my disciple-faculty of strength.
I AM strong in the Lord.

Now, from the strength center, bring your focus of attention forward to the solar plexus. (It is just below your rib cage, in the center of your body.)

Remember that *solar* means sun and *plexus* means center: the sun center, the center of light and wisdom. Affirm:

Christ in me calls forth James,
the son of Zebedee,
my disciple-faculty of
wisdom and good judgment.

After a time conclude with the thought:

I AM grateful!

The color key for wisdom is yellow, as you might guess from its frequent comparison to the sun.

LOVE

John—Behind the Heart

The disciple John represents the faculty of love.

The place in the physical body that Charles Fillmore designates as the throne, or seat, or center of the faculty or power of love is the network of nerves just behind the heart.

The disciples John and James were brothers. Jesus called them "the sons of thunder!"

The physical centers for the faculties of love (John) and wisdom (James) are very close together and joined by bundles of nerves. James, or wisdom, you will remember, presides over the solar plexus region. The dictionary describes the solar plexus as, "The large network of sympathetic nerves and ganglia located in the cavity behind the stomach."

Let me repeat, John and James were brothers; notice the especially close relationship between the love center just behind the heart and the wisdom center just behind the stomach.

Not only are they physically close, but these physical centers are interrelated. For instance, whatever affects the stomach will sympathetically affect the heart, and vice versa. People with weak stomachs or indigestion often think they have heart trouble. There is a very definite and strong physiological tie between these two body centers, just as there is a strong bond between the faculties of love and wisdom.

We may think from the head, but we feel from the solar plexus—heart region. Feeling is that which gives the real power to thought!

I once watched a television program in which Willie Mays was honored. His interviewer remarked with admiration, "Willie Mays is someone you can trust. He speaks from the gut!"

That means, obviously, that he speaks with feeling (solar plexus) and with sincerity (heart).

As you speak the Christ word of truth to spiritually quicken these two brother centers, your environment will reflect the powerful vibrations that they command. You will understand why they are called "sons of thunder"!

But now let's talk in a little more depth about love.

One of the reasons we get into much of the trouble that keeps us tense, worried, and crawling the walls is that we ignorantly divorce or separate love from wisdom.

The two must go together in order to give the balance necessary for harmonious and wholesome expression.

Divorce is a good descriptive word to clarify this area, for Charles Fillmore states that ideas have a sex (meaning gender). He writes, "The evidence that sex exists in the vegetable and animal worlds is so clear that it is never questioned, but we have not so clearly discerned that ideas are also male and female."

Love, as a universal idea, is feminine. Wisdom, as a universal idea, is masculine. They need to be together; they belong together.

When love is divorced from or not united with wisdom, it gets into all kinds of trouble.

Love can become a "patsy," a "vampire," a fanatic, a dictator, or a cunning manipulator.

Love without wisdom can be an "easy mark."

We all know people who don't have the courage and wisdom to say "no." They are forever wearing themselves out doing things for others, rationalizing it as love, but inwardly resenting it. You can tell it was counterfeit love when they complain in self-pity, "After all I have done, how could they treat me like that?"

Love without wisdom can be a vampire!

A vampire uses people. Remember how the classic Dracula would be so kind, gracious, charming, and thoughtful to his victims, then drain their life-energy from them?

Did you ever get "used" by vampire love? Someone flattered and praised you, and put you on a pedestal as if you were a hero or heroine. Of course, what you didn't realize is that this person lost nothing in placing you on the pedestal; it made him or her greater than you. For is not someone who is responsible for making a hero greater than the hero?

At any rate, you then, out of your royal position, are obligated to bestow whatever favor is asked by the one who made you the hero. Then came the emotional and sometimes physical and financial draining. A person driven by ambition knows this vampire technique well.

Love without wisdom can be fanatical.

Hitler "loved" Germany, and his love brought tragedy and unspeakable carnage.

The Church-sanctioned "soldiers" of the Inquisition loved Jesus and the Church so much that they felt it was actually good and right to torture people to join the Christian religion.

Ah, yes. Love without wisdom can be fanatical.

Love without wisdom can be a self-deceiver. Parents who poke their noses into the lives of their grown children, with resulting emotional pain and discord, will deceive themselves that they are good and blameless because they did it out of love for the children.

Or love can be a dictator. A father gave his young son a train set. The father felt that the purpose of a train set was to have it run like a real train—on the tracks, switching cars, stopping at stations, and so forth.

However, from the youngster's point of view, the purpose of a train set was to see the wonderful "craaaaash" as it went off the tracks or barreled into another car.

The father scolded the child until he abruptly realized that if this were a real love-gift, it must be without strings. He had no right to enforce his idea of the purpose of a train set on the one he "gave" it to.

Perhaps we could argue about the example,

but the principle of dictator-love or dictator-giving is a favorite cover-up in many more subtle ways of ego-satisfaction.

I trust that from what we have discussed you can see that love without wisdom is like playing with electricity without knowing how to control or direct it. You may do some good, or you may innocently or ignorantly blow all the fuses.

And now to the meditation exercise.

After acknowledging that the Christ of God is quickened in you (you can refer to the previous lessons in this series for the suggested way in which this is done), bring your attention to the middle of your head, specifically the pineal gland, which is the physical center for the faculty of faith, represented by Peter. Silently affirm:

Christ in me quickens the disciple-faculty of faith. I have faith in God so that when I say to a mountainous challenge, "Be thou removed!" I do not doubt in my heart, and that which I say is done.

Next, let your attention travel to your strength center at the small of your back, just below the ribs and above the pelvis, and silently affirm:

Christ in me quickens the disciple-faculty of strength in me.

A Twelve-Power Meditation Exercise

I am strong in the Lord
and in the power of His might!
Now focus on the wisdom center in the solar
plexus and affirm:
Christ in me quickens the
disciple-faculty of wisdom in me.
I am in tune with the
infinite wisdom of universal mind.
And now bring the focal point of your
attention up just a bit to the area behind the
heart, the love center. Affirm these thoughts:
Christ in me quickens the disciple-faculty of
love in me. I am a radiating center of pure,
unadulterated love; mighty to attract my good,
and to radiate good to others. (Love, you see,
has a magnetic quality to it. It is an attracting,
cohesive power.)

Now remember that love and wisdom go
together as powerhouse sons of thunder.
Gratefully acknowledge that they are
quickened in you.

Close your meditation with the "Prayer for
Protection" by James Dillet Freeman:
The light of God surrounds me;
The love of God enfolds me;
The power of God protects me;
The presence of God watches over me.
Wherever I am, God is!
The color key for love is pink. Think pink.

POWER

Philip—Throat

"To know the pains of power, we must go to those who have it; to know its pleasures, we must go to those who are seeking it: the pains of power are real, its pleasures imaginary."

C.C. Colton

This is well put; it clearly points out the futility of the world's concept of power—power over other people, power to control people and circumstances.

Power promises pleasure and fulfillment, but ends up with pain, guilt, and loneliness.

Not so with the power we are talking about in this lesson. It is not power exercised over others; rather it is a quickening of the power-faculty in you, which allows the universal power of God to move through you.

Our premise for this Twelve-Power Meditation series is that Jesus and His disciples symbolize the Christ in you and the twelve faculties or powers of mind through which the Christ expresses.

An analogy might be a huge business which has a head or president, and twelve department heads, each of whom has a different type of work, but each of whom also needs to cooperate with the others in perfectly and efficiently carrying out the policy or directives of the president of the company.

Jesus taught and trained His twelve disciples. In this meditation exercise, seek to let the Christ in you call forth, train, and quicken your twelve faculties of mind.

Charles Fillmore's book, *The Twelve Powers of Man*, is our source book; but instead of just dealing with the concept in an intellectual way, we are endeavoring to translate the intellectually stated principles into a personal application. In short, we add doing to listening or reading.

And now for the faculty of power.

The disciple who represents power is Philip. The name *Philip* is from the Greek, and means "lover of horses." Horsepower is a common unit of measurement for energy or power.

The physical center of power in the body is the throat, or more specifically, the root of the tongue.

Charles Fillmore writes, "The power center in the throat controls all the vibratory energies of the organism. It is the open door between the formless and the formed worlds of vibrations pertaining to the expression of sound."

Think about this for a moment. Many times you have thoughts and feelings surging around in you which are, of course, formless, invisible; but then your mind shapes them into words, and gives an order to a network of nerves that stimulate the muscles in your throat in an incomprehensibly complicated way—and out come your thoughts in "sound capsules" called words!

Now every word as it passes through this magic, miracle door receives a "charge" of power! The character of that charge, positive or negative, is determined by the consciousness of the individual.

For instance, if the overall tenor of a person's consciousness is one of selfish ambition, or greed, or fear, or inferiority, this will be the character of the "power charge" inserted or impregnated in his or her words.

You only have to listen to a person speak for five minutes and you receive a very good idea of what kind of person he or she is. It isn't so much what is said; it is the way it is said—the feeling you get from the speaker.

However, when you seek, through meditation, to let the Christ instead of the personal ego guide, govern, and direct your thoughts and feelings, a charge of spiritual power is implanted or infused in your every word.

This is the deeper meaning of Jesus' statement, "It is the spirit that gives life, the flesh is of no avail; the words that I have spoken to you are spirit and life" (Jn. 6:63). "Heaven and earth will pass away, but my words will not pass away" (Mt. 24:35).

As you work with the meditation exercise, you will find more and more spiritual power being infused into the words that come through the power center, the doorway from the unformed to the formed, the throat.

This accounts for that mysterious something that makes a singer great. Or, to quote Charles Fillmore again, "Voice culture may give one tone brilliancy, but every great singer has the soul contact."

However, the power-faculty does not and

must not work alone, as Paul points out: "If I speak in the tongues of men and of angels, but have not love, I am a noisy gong or a clanging cymbal" (1 Cor. 13:1).

But power working with the love center behind the heart makes your words a powerful harmonizing influence.

Power working with the faith center at the pineal gland in the head gives your words the mountain-moving power that Jesus spoke of when He said, "If you have faith and never doubt . . . if you say to this mountain, 'Be taken up and cast into the sea,' it will be done" (Mt. 21:21).

We know that words can travel long distances, even around the world, when converted into an electrical impulse. Today they bound these electrical impulses off satellites in space and the impulses rebound into homes half a world away.

What our limited thinking is not yet able to conceive and believe is that spiritually charged words do not need a medium to wing their way around the world faster than the speed of light.

Charles Fillmore wrote that words of Truth generate a vibration which, like the circles made when you throw a pebble into a pool, go around the world.

A Twelve-Power Meditation Exercise

I remembered his words when I was a
student minister. I had never studied public
speaking, nor did it come naturally or easily to
me. All the books said, "Look your audience in
the eye when you talk!"

Well, I just couldn't. I could talk to just one
person, but if I would switch my complete
attention to another person as the book
advised, it would be like starting over and I
would lose a sense of sincerity.

So, public speaking rules or not, when I
speak, I think of Charles Fillmore and feel that
the words go right through the walls of the
building to help in some way the entire
world—including those who are listening close
by.

Before we get into the meditation phase of
the lesson, I want to be sure that you do not
interpret anything I say to mean that spiritual
power means to speak in a loud or com-
manding voice.

People who talk loudly and boldly are often
inwardly insecure, and the loud talk is a screen
to keep others off guard so they don't see the
loud talker's fear.

Spiritual power is quiet, smooth, flowing,
harmonious. Or, as Solomon put it in Proverbs
25:15: "A soft tongue will break a bone."

And now the meditation exercise.

From the four previous lessons, you remember the first part of the exercise in which you place your center of attention at the crown of the head, then the forehead, then the solar plexus to acknowledge the quickening of the Christ in you.

In this lesson we are going to relate the power faculty to the four faculties we have previously studied: faith, strength, wisdom, and love.

Relax, be aware of your breathing, go within.

After the first part of the exercise mentioned above, focalize your attention at the base of the tongue or the throat area, and silently say or think:

> *The Christ in me calls forth Philip,*
> *my disciple-faculty of power. The*
> *words that I speak are Spirit and*
> *life, and do accomplish that*
> *whereto they are sent.*

Next, let that focal point of attention travel upward to the faith center in the pineal gland in the head and know:

> *My quickened faith in God gives*
> *my words mountain-moving power.*

Now drop your attention to the small of your back, the strength center:

> *My strength is sustained by*

*the power of Spirit. I do
not weaken or falter.*

Next, concentrate on the solar plexus, and affirm:

*Infinite wisdom imbues my word
with intuitive ability to get
to the heart of the matter.*

Now move upward slightly to the love center, the back of the heart, and silently whisper:

*The power of love casts out
all fear and breaks
through all barriers.*

Close your meditation by speaking the "Prayer for Protection," and as you do, feel that a white light is flowing down over your entire body from the crown of your head to a few inches below your feet.

The light of God surrounds me;

The love of God enfolds me;

The power of God protects me;

The presence of God watches over me.

Wherever I am, God is!

The color that is identified with power is purple. Kings wear royal purple as a symbol of power.

IMAGINATION

Bartholomew—Between the Eyes

"Divine imagination is the chisel we wield in molding the paradise of our inner thought kingdoms."—Cora Fillmore, *Christ Enthroned in Man*.

Cora Fillmore likens the imagination to a chisel; other Truth teachers have called it "the scissors of the mind."

Scissors in the hands of a skilled dressmaker cut out a perfectly fitting dress. Scissors in the hands of a novice will probably waste a lot of material and even then come up with an ill-fitting outfit.

It is important that you recognize the importance of your mental faculty of imagination and know how to use it skillfully in molding the mental forms for the outer expression of your needs and desires.

The disciple Bartholomew represents the faculty of imagination. The physical center in the body is directly between the eyes. Charles Fillmore writes, "This is the point of expression for a set of tissues that extend back into the brain and connect with an imaging or picture-making function near the root of the optic nerve."

Perhaps you are familiar with this area between the eyes as being the location some call "the third eye."

At any rate, we all know that when you close your eyes to daydream, or to mentally rerun an episode from the past, you "watch" the "film" supplied by the subconscious mind through this area between and a little above the eyes.

Now here is a very interesting and eye-opening fact about the imagination: under certain conditions the influence of the imagination can overcome or "cut out" the visual image coming through the physical eyes.

In other words, it is possible for you to see not what is actually there, but what you want to see.

It is also possible to see things not as they

are, but as someone or some circumstance strongly suggests that you see them.

Let me repeat that because it is thought provoking: it is possible for the faculty of imagination, with its physical center between the eyes, to overcome or "cut out" the actual visual image coming through the physical eyes, and to send another picture to the brain. You, of course, are certain that the picture from the imagination is real.

Let me give you a perfect example of this.

Kreskin, a famous mentalist, was giving a public performance. He had forty people on stage who were strongly suggestible. He told them that a man impersonating Sid Collins, the announcer for the Indianapolis 500 race, was going to come on stage. However, Kreskin said, or suggested, that Sid would be dressed shabbily, his clothes would be soiled, and he would smell bad.

Well, Sid Collins came on stage, dressed in his usual exceptionally good taste. But the forty people on stage treated him in accordance with the way Kreskin had described him. They openly showed their displeasure and revulsion; in fact four of the men tried to bodily carry him off stage and had to be restrained!

Later Sid told me that one of the persons who had acted thus was a personal friend. Sid asked him, "Tell me honestly, what did I look like to you at that time?"

The friend replied very frankly that he actually saw him in an old and torn shirt and worn, baggy pants. Actually Sid Collins not only was well-dressed, but he was wearing a sport coat.

This is an overpowering example of how a strong suggestion to a suggestible mind actually cuts off the outer image and substitutes an image that the mind, through the faculty of imagination, feels is more in line with the outer suggestion that the mind had totally accepted.

Of course, this opens up new avenues of thought about apparitions people see. Are they seen through the physical eye, or does a strong suggestion, or a deep desire and emotional need to see a certain form or event override the physical eye and substitute the desired or suggested image?

The imagining faculty, or what we commonly call "our imagination," has long been underestimated. It is tolerated in children and accepted as a kind of "secret hideaway" for adults, called daydreaming or fantasizing one's desires. But it is not quite as innocent and powerless as we may have thought.

The imagination is a universal language, for it is a language of pictures. A picture of a cup of water, for instance, is understood by people of every language. Jesus taught spiritual principles through parables which are pictures. The pictures of the prodigal son tiring of a life of poverty and bondage and returning to his father is the same picture, no matter in what language you hear the parable.

This brings us to the faculty of imagination as an all-important means of communication from universal Mind, or God, to you and to me.

In biblical days the prophets received prophecies, warnings, and wisdom through visions and dreams—all functions of the faculty of imagination.

Joseph interpreted the Pharaoh's dream of the seven lean and seven fat cattle. Daniel correctly described and interpreted Nebuchadnezzar's dream. To quote the Bible: "Then the mystery was revealed to Daniel in a vision of the night" (Dan. 2:19).

However, in each case the faculty of understanding was equally developed. Understanding is the next power of mind that we study and insert into our Twelve-Power Meditation technique; but that is for the next lesson.

The point is that when you quicken and spiritualize your faculty of imagination, or

rather, when you affirm and acknowledge that
the Christ in you is quickening the faculty of
imagination in you, it becomes the channel of
communication between you and universal
Mind.

Through the universal language of pictures
you see new ways to solve old problems. You
see new ways of doing your work more
efficiently and successfully. You develop what
is called a creative imagination.

Einstein said, "Imagination is more important
than knowledge."

The imagination "sees" the completed event,
condition, or form, and that mental image acts
as a magnet for the slower moving knowledge.

Now, with a new appreciation for your
faculty of imagination, let us include it in the
Twelve-Power Meditation.

Take a few moments to relax and enjoy
inner quietness.

Then, with the center of attention at the
crown of your head, affirm:

The Christ of God is
quickened in me.

Moving to the forehead, to acknowledge that
you are aware or conscious of this spiritual
awakening, affirm:

I am aware that the Christ
of God is quickened in me.

Now to the solar plexus region, the
emotional center, feel the emotion of gratitude
in response to this Christ quickening. Affirm:
> *I am grateful that the Christ*
> *of God is quickened in me.*

Move your center of attention to the middle
of your head, the pineal gland, the physical
center for faith, represented by Peter:
> *I am developing mountain-moving*
> *faith in God.*

Then move to the small of your back, the
physical center of strength, represented by
Andrew, and affirm:
> *My faith in God makes me strong*
> *and of good courage.*

Then to the wisdom area at the solar plexus,
represented by James, affirm:
> *I am guided by wisdom and good*
> *judgment into right action.*

Now to the love center, an area behind the
heart, represented by the beloved disciple,
John, affirm:
> *I am filled and thrilled with*
> *the magnetic forces of love.*

The power center is next, the throat or base
of the tongue, represented by the disciple
Philip. Affirm:
> *I am power!*

Now to Bartholomew, who represents

imagination, with your center of attention between the eyes, affirm:

> *Christ in me quickens my*
> *faculty of imagination.*
> *I see clearly and creatively.*

Conclude your meditation by repeating the "Prayer for Protection" and feel yourself bathed in light:

> The light of God surrounds me;
> The love of God enfolds me;
> The power of God protects me;
> The presence of God watches over me.
> Wherever I am, God is!

The color coordinate is light blue, the color of the early morning sky in summer.

UNDERSTANDING AND WILL

Thomas (Understanding)
Matthew (Will)—Forehead

"With all thy getting get understanding" (Prov. 4:7 AV).

"The will is the man" wrote nineteenth-century mystic John Wilson in his *Noctes Ambrosianae*.

What is this understanding, the getting of which is more to be desired than rubies or precious gems? Why is the will the person?

In this lesson we study the mind power faculties of understanding and will together, for we find they are so closely related. The will is the executive department; it carries out, or executes, what you understand to be right and good, or at any rate, what you understand to be your best course of action.

Understanding is represented by the disciple Thomas; will is represented by the disciple Matthew. The location in the physical body for both of these disciple-faculties is the forehead.

The reason for taking them together is that they work as a team: the will carries out what we understand or accept as true.

Cora Fillmore writes: "These powers working together have the ability to perceive in the invisible realm of thought [understanding], and to direct and bring the inner light from the unmanifest to the manifest world [will]."

In short, these are your faculties of mind that connect the inner world of thought to the outer world of manifestation. You do, you act, you execute what your predominant thought or thoughts are.

To be specific—if your thoughts are predominantly materialistic, worshiping money and power, then your actions are directed toward cultivating influential friends, reading financial statements, studying ways of making more money or increasing your investments.

Or to put it in exaggerated form, someone who thinks about golf all the time doesn't "will" to spend his leisure time playing tennis.

He "wills" or acts out his "golf thoughts."

Now, there are two kinds of understanding: intellectual understanding and spiritual understanding.

Intellectual understanding is garnered from outside yourself through your five senses.

Spiritual understanding wells up from within you through intuition and inspiration.

Intellectual understanding isn't bad; it is incomplete. When your understanding is incomplete your actions are bound to be prone to error.

Let me give you an example of how incompleteness is not bad but can be a handicap.

There are three dimensions to all form: length, breadth, and depth. Say that you were only able to perceive two dimensions, length and breadth. What a confusing situation it would be to see how tall and how wide an object was, but not even be aware of it having depth. What you saw was true and good, but you weren't seeing it all.

Thus it is with intellectual and spiritual understanding. Intellectual understanding; that is, what you see, what you read, what you hear from teachers, parents, friends, is part of the picture, part of the material on which you base your actions. But in order to get the whole picture and therefore make sure you are taking right action, you should take advantage of your inner senses of intuition and inspiration in order to receive light or guidance from universal wisdom.

I have always found the metaphysical interpretation of John the Baptist interesting and revealing. John the Baptist represents intellectual understanding; Jesus represents spiritual understanding.

John the Baptist came first; but he knew that he wasn't the answer, the light; he was a forerunner whose work it was to point to the light to come.

Even so, many Truth students have found the answers they have been seeking in Truth books. They eagerly fill their intellectual understanding with scads of information about Truth, about God, about spiritual laws and principles. They build up an intellectual vocabulary of spiritual terms or jargon, such as: infinite Mind, Christ in me, one Presence and one Power, divine Love, and the rest.

This is good, but it is incomplete. John the Baptist pointed the way, but he was not the way. Intellectual understanding or information about Truth points the way, but it is not *the way*.

The complete way is to go within in

meditation to let your inner self bask in the light of spiritual understanding. Then the will expresses understanding into the outer world that includes both the intellectual knowledge or information along with the spiritual inspiration or intuitive guidance.

Once you begin to spiritually quicken your faculty of understanding, it may rearrange your entire structure of values. For instance, say you have been programmed; that is, you have received from the outer world (parents, general observation) the thought that success is of great importance, and to be a success you must win over the other guy—by fair means, if possible—but win.

In meditation, spiritual understanding may make crystal clear to you that these goals are misleading, that the success they bring is hollow and empty, because they stem from wrong motives of greed, ambition, pride, and vanity.

This is not to say that spiritually oriented individuals are losers or failures or poverty stricken; for when you seek to let the light of understanding motivate and guide you, its proclivity is always toward increase—toward the increase of beauty, harmony, needed supply, inner peace, and fulfillment.

Just one more point before we get to the

meditation. We have talked about the faculty
of imagination and its physical location
between the eyes. You will notice that all three
faculty centers—will, understanding, and
imagination—are very close together, and not
just physically close.

For instance, usually we think (understanding) in pictures (imagination).

A basketball player can imagine shooting the
ball through the hoop, and in actual play the
will (the executive branch, or faculty) acts out
the imagined picture, and the player's skill
increases.

Also, the imagination can overrule
understanding. If you were blindfolded and
told that the foot-wide board you were walking
on was fifty feet in the air, even though you
knew this was not so, you would feel tinges of
fear and might even lose your balance.

Your understanding says everything is okay,
but your imagination says you might possibly
be fifty feet up on a narrow board (after all
you are blindfolded). The imagination
overrules the understanding and the will obeys
the imagination; you perspire, tremble a bit,
and get weak in the knees.

Yes, it is significant that these three faculties
are closely related in every way.

Now the meditation.

Relax . . . and sigh.

Then, with the center of attention at the crown of the head, affirm:

The Christ of God is
quickened in me.

Moving to the forehead, to acknowledge that you are aware or conscious of this spiritual awakening, affirm:

I am aware that the Christ
of God is quickened in me.

Now to the solar plexus region, the emotional center, feel the emotion of gratitude in response to this Christ quickening. Affirm:

I am grateful that the Christ
of God is quickened in me.

Now gently and easily let the focus or spotlight of your attention travel to each of the physical centers we have studied:

Faith (Pineal gland in the head)

Strength (Small of back)

Wisdom (Solar plexus)

Love (Behind the heart)

Power (Base of throat)

Imagination (Between the eyes).

Now let your attention rest at the forehead and spiritually quicken the faculties of under-standing and will by affirming:

The light of understanding enables me to see
clearly and to take right action.

Conclude your meditation with the "Prayer for Protection" and feel that you are standing in a shower of light as you speak the words:

The light of God surrounds me;
The love of God enfolds me;
The power of God protects me;
The presence of God watches over me.
Wherever I am, God is!

Note: You may have noticed that in each of the lessons the meditations have been slightly different. Sometimes we use different statements for the various disciple-faculties, and sometimes we vary the structure of the meditation itself.

This has been done purposely in order to point out that you should not feel that the statements I suggest are the only ones to use. Use words that feel right to you.

The color that coordinates with understanding is gold. The color that coordinates with will is silver.

ORDER

James, the son of Alphaeus—Navel

In the chapter on order in Charles Fillmore's book *The Twelve Powers of Man*, he explains the Unity concept of the "only begotten Son."

I think it will be helpful at this point to thoughtfully consider his interpretation, which is very much different from the traditional interpretation handed down to us from the Middle Ages.

John 3:16 states, "God so loved the world that he gave his only Son, that whoever believes in him should not perish but have eternal life." Fillmore writes, "This does not mean that a

personal man named Jesus of Nazareth was
sent forth as a special propitiation for the sins
of the world, or that the only available route
into the Father's presence lies through such a
person. It simply means that God has provided
a way by which all men may come consciously
into His presence in their own souls. That way
is through the only begotten Son of God, the
Christ consciousness, which Jesus demonstrated. This consciousness is the always
present Son of the Father, dwelling as a
spiritual seed in each of us and ready to
germinate and grow at our will."

This establishes the basis for the Twelve-
Power Meditation. We understand the Christ in
us to be a spiritual seed, and in meditation we
are willing to let that seed, that spiritual
organic process, germinate and grow.

Just as Jesus' first action was to call twelve
disciples to assist Him in carrying out His
work, so do we, in meditation, call forth or
quicken the twelve powers or faculties of mind
through which the Christ seed in us grows and
expresses.

You find that each of Jesus' disciples
represents one of the twelve powers of mind.
The following are the disciples, the mind
powers they represent, and the physical centers
in the body presided over by each faculty-

disciple that we have studied to date in this
series:
Peter—faith—the pineal gland in the middle of
the head;
Andrew—strength—the small of the back;
John—love—behind the heart;
James—wisdom—the solar plexus;
Philip—power—the root of the tongue or
throat;
Bartholomew—imagination—between the eyes;
Thomas—understanding—the forehead;
Matthew—will—the forehead.

And now to the faculty of order.

James, the son of Alphaeus (sometimes called
James the Less), represents the faculty of order.
The physical center is a ganglionic center of
nerves back of the navel. The navel is the place
where the umbilical cord is attached to the
newly forming infant. Here is how the
dictionary describes this important connection:

"The umbilical cord is a flexible, cordlike
structure that connects the fetus at the navel
with the placenta, and it contains two
umbilical arteries and one vein that nourish
and feed the fetus and remove the waste."

The navel then is a control center. Before
birth the control of the nourishment and
elimination of waste, the basics of growth, are
administered in an orderly way from the

mother through the umbilical cord.

Upon birth into the outer world, the cord is severed and the control becomes inner directed.

We think, then, of the faculty of order as a control center for the individual's growth—physically, mentally, and spiritually.

Its office or responsibility is to control the orderliness, harmony, and right timing of the growing or unfolding process.

The faculty of order is the department that makes things go right, and not only right, but smoothly, effortlessly, harmoniously.

Let's use an analogy to make this clear.

Think of the faculty of order as having the job that a stage manager has in the theater.

As you watch a play unfold, everything seems to go so smoothly, naturally, and easily. Perhaps one of the actors picks up a picture from a table on the stage and makes a remark about it. It seems very natural, but who arranged for the picture to be there, and the right picture at that?

Or suppose the phone rings on stage just as one of the actors is at a certain place in his lines. Who arranged for the phone to ring just then?

We could go on with examples all through the play, but you get the idea. The stage manager sees that everything unfolds in the right way with perfect timing, for the harmonious unfoldment of the story.

This is how the disciple-faculty of order assists the unfolding Christ in you. When you persistently affirm in meditation that the faculty of order is being spiritually quickened, you find divine order being established in your mind, body, and life.

You are in the right place at the right time to learn what you need to learn, or to do what needs to be done by you at that particular place in your unfoldment.

Divine order is established in your bodily functions, which means, of course, health.

The faculty of order is very sensitive and will respond quickly when you turn a situation over to its control. You can test this for yourself. The next time everything seems to go wrong, and you feel confused and at wit's end, affirm divine order. Get the help of your spiritual stage manager to set things right.

Right into the teeth of the confusing facts that are staring you in the face, say calmly:

All is in divine order.

First there is a response in you, a kind of relaxing of tension, a lifting of a weight. When you look back at the episode you will find that that moment was the turning point when things began to shape up and go smoothly once more.

Order, you see, is law. The words *law* and *order* go together.

When you break a civil law, you are fined or imprisoned. It is thought of and experienced as punishment, but the true purpose is corrective.

Likewise, when you ignorantly or compulsively break divine law (that is, when you get out of tune or out of order with universal harmony), you find yourself imprisoned by circumstances; or something you valued is unexpectedly withheld from you.

We always claim we are innocent, of course, just as most of those who break civil laws claim that they are innocent, or make excuses that circumstances forced them into doing what they did.

However, when we unwittingly or otherwise break divine law, wise people regard the seemingly unpleasant effect not as punishment, but as corrective. And we seek, as quickly as possible, to get back in tune with God by affirming divine order.

To close this lesson on order, relax and turn within.

Ignore for the moment the sounds and sights, the outer stimuli coming in through the senses. Become aware of that vast universe of inner space in which you and I and all persons live and move and have awareness and being.

Let your center of attention drop easily to a point just behind the navel, the physical center for the faculty of order.

Say or think to yourself:

> *Christ in me is quickening my*
> *faculty of order, represented*
> *by the disciple James, the*
> *son of Alphaeus.*

Then, holding your attention there, affirm:

> *Divine order is established*
> *in my mind, body, and life.*

And you may wish to add:

> *I AM in tune with divine timing,*
> *and I let God create this day for me.*

Now, during the day when your plans are changed unexpectedly, or you find yourself knotted up with tension, quickly let your attention go to the navel area and say:

> *Divine order—I am in tune*
> *with divine order.*

The color associated with order is green, the rich, deep green of mid-August trees, as opposed to light green, which is associated with the faculty of strength.

ZEAL

Simon, the Zealot—
Medulla, Back of Head

Zeal is a necessary faculty of mind, but it is also very sensitive, easily misunderstood and misused.

It has been said that: "Zeal is fit only for wise Men, but is found mostly in Fools!"—Thomas Fuller, M.D., 1732.

Charles Fillmore placed the physical center for the faculty of zeal at the medulla of the brain; that is, the base of the brain or the back of the neck.

This would seem to be logical, for many of us are familiar with those back-of-the-neck tension headaches that usually follow a period of activity when we are emotionally upset, anxious, fearful of failure, or impatient.

In these instances, our faculty of zeal is unwisely used and results in a short circuit of power, causing congestion and stress at the zeal center.

Yes, zeal is a sensitive faculty, and unless it is under the direction of the indwelling Christ, it is prone to "boil over."

The disciple who represents zeal is Simon. In the New Testament, he is sometimes called Simon the Zealot, and at other times Simon the Canaanite.

Zeal is the faculty of mind that gives us "go power." Zeal is energy; it is the push that drives us toward our goal in spite of obstacles or hindrances.

Zeal is ardor, enthusiasm, persistence, motivation. We need to develop this important disciple-faculty, and learn how to use it rightly.

Countless people lead mediocre lives because they lack ability to persevere. They may "catch fire" with a certain project or idea, but the fire soon burns out, and these people return to their routine, challenge-free lives.

This is because their faculty of zeal is motivated not by an inner spark, but by some outer suggestion or excitement. We see an example of this in high-powered sales meetings or rallies.

A Twelve-Power Meditation Exercise

The meeting hall is filled with posters, slogans, and pictures of the smiling and prosperous founder of the business organization. These all are what psychologists call signals, or suggestions.

Then follow emotion arousing songs that appeal to the personal ego, with words such as, "We are number one!" or "We will win no matter what the odds!" Then come fantastic testimonials that stir up the subconscious green "demon" of jealousy: "If they can do it, so can I. I'll show them!"

This is negative motivation. It is all outer-suggested motivation, and thereby counterfeit, and temporary at best. The hyped-up sales-persons go out aflame with zeal and enthusiasm; but gradually as they knock on door after door it fizzles out . . . until the next happy, handclapping sales meeting.

Inner-motivated zeal is constant, durable, persistent—because it flows from a spiritual source within you.

The word *zeal* is many times associated with a wild-eyed, intense, fanatic person. This is because it is so universally misused.

True zeal is quiet, continuous, patient, persevering in a calm way in spite of events, people, or circumstances that would distract it.

Zeal, when its motivation is from within, is

like the song, "Old Man River," it just keeps rollin' along. Dependable is another description of zeal, and you know how much dependable people are admired and sought after.

As you bless and quicken your faculty of zeal and commit it to the control and direction of the Christ within, you will find yourself with boundless energy, never tiring, but always active—unhurried, graceful, gracious, persistent.

But now let's talk a bit more about the physical center of zeal in the body: the medulla, or if you prefer, the medulla oblongata—the base of the brain.

The medulla sits right on top of the spinal column at the base of the brain. Its function is to handle the messages from and give orders to the circulatory and respiratory systems, and also to the heart and other involuntary functions.

Here again it is interesting to note how Charles Fillmore's intuitive insight seems so logical and correct. He wrote: "Jesus had two apostles named Simon, but they represent different talents or faculties of man's mind. Simon Peter represents receptivity from above [faith], and Simon the Cananaean represents receptivity from below. The Canaanites dwelt in the lowlands, so we know that the faculty designated by Simon the Cananaean has its origin in the body consciousness."

Sure enough, we see that the medulla, the physical center for Simon the Cananaean, responds to and deals with the subconscious body functions, such as breathing, the beating of the heart, and the contraction and expansion of the arteries and blood vessels.

When we are excited, impatient, or angry, our breathing is affected; it becomes shallow and hurried.

When we allow emotional states to take over in our field of consciousness, or mind, they short-circuit this critical and sensitive center, causing the blood vessels to contract and resulting in back-of-the-head headaches. The emotions of guilt or jealousy are particularly destructive in this way.

Under severe emotional stress some people faint. Fainting, too, has to do with the medulla. It is often caused by cutting off the blood supply.

We can begin to see how intimately the faculty of zeal with its center in the medulla is tied to our emotional response to what happens to and around us.

This is why it is so important to develop what I like to call "a center of calmness." When excitement and stimulation from the environment tempt us to react with emotion, we are able to retreat to the center of calmness within for that split second that it takes to abort the compulsive emotional response, and to maintain poise and patience so that we can take positive action.

Thus, we not only make a wise and right response to the outer event or condition, but we save all the stress and actual pain that the body must absorb as a repercussion of a violent emotional response.

Yes, zeal is a tremendously important faculty of mind. When we combine spiritual zeal with faith, our reliance on God never wavers. When we combine spiritual zeal with love, love becomes enduring in spite of faults or blemishes. When we combine spiritual zeal with imagination, our creativity is not chained to a certain place or time or mood, but gushes forth at our beck and call.

It is important to combine wisdom and understanding with spiritual zeal; this is the secret of genius. Remember that zeal is fit only for the wise.

Now let's get into the meditation part of the lesson.

Remember, this Twelve-Power Meditation technique is distinctive in that we involve all dimensions of the threefold being that humankind is: the spiritual, the mental, and the physical.

It is spiritual because we are acknowledging the presence in us of the image-likeness of God, the Christ. It is mental in that we are consciously directing our thoughts in a spiritual framework. It is physical in that we focus the attention on a specific center in the body.

Now relax and close your eyes.

For a moment enjoy resting your eyes on that dark field of velvety blackness into which you seem to be gazing. (Actually it is probably the back of your eyelids, but it is also a transition point, a jumping-off point into the depths of inner consciousness.)

Now let your attention go to the back of your neck. Let it rest there for a moment, like a soft, golden circle of light.

Then say or think silently:

> *The Christ within me is quick-*
> *ening, baptizing, and training*
> *my faculty of zeal, repre-*
> *sented by the disciple Simon,*
> *the Cananaean.*

Immediately you will feel a sense of peace, an easing of tension: your breathing will respond by getting deeper and more rhythmic. Perhaps there will even be a sigh of relief and release.

Now affirm:

I am motivated from within by wisdom and love. I do that which is before me to do with unflagging zeal and enthusiasm. I work with the spring and speed of Spirit—easily, unhurriedly, gracefully. I am grateful.

Thomas a Kempis, in *Of the Imitation of Christ*, wrote: "We are often moved with passion, and we think it to be zeal."

Remember, passion is motivated by outer people, events, or conditions; zeal is motivated by the spirit of God in us when we are calm and receptive.

The color associated with the faculty of zeal is orange. This, too, agrees with logic, for the color orange is exciting and stimulating.

RENUNCIATION

Thaddaeus—Lower Spine

The faculty of renunciation is represented by the disciple Thaddaeus.

The area of the body governed by this faculty is the lowest part of the back, at the base of the spinal column.

Fillmore, in the book *The Twelve Powers of Man*, is more specific in his definition. He writes: "The apostle Thaddaeus . . . carries forward the work of elimination of error thoughts from the mind and of waste food from the body. The nerve center . . . is located deep in the lower bowels."

Now to some, and certainly to myself, when I first read Fillmore's book, this

seemed a little—how should I say
it?—indelicate, something that isn't talked
about. Yet, if we clear out of our minds all the
no-no's that well-meaning but puritanically
modest persons have laid on us, we can
understand how the faculty of renunciation or
elimination is not only very important, but it is
good, clean, and tremendously necessary in
both a mental and physical way.

The idea of renunciation or elimination as a
mental power or faculty is new to most of us,
so let's name a few of the functions and
characteristics of this faculty.

Under the office of renunciation come the
subdepartments of release, letting go, and
relaxation. You know how important these
mental attitudes are.

Let go your fears and doubts, and let God.
As we quicken and spiritually train the
Thaddaeus faculty, we find it easier to relax
and let go.

Also under the Thaddaeus disciple of
renunciation we have the activities of
cleansing, purifying, purging of that which is
worn out or no longer useful and therefore is
detrimental.

I remember reading many years ago of a
scientific experiment with a single cell.
Scientists found that the secret of keeping the

cell alive and healthy is to make sure that all the waste given off by the cell is removed. With all their apparatus they couldn't find a way of completely removing all the waste. They concluded that if such a way were to be discovered there was no reason why the cell shouldn't stay alive and healthy forever.

In short, this faculty of elimination is an important factor in the regeneration of the physical body.

Many of you remember how parents years ago would say, "Give the child some castor oil," when you exhibited symptoms of illness. This was to get rid of body poisons in nature's own way.

Just as the idea of elimination is important in the health and regeneration of the body, so it is necessary in the mind. Fillmore writes: "There must be a renunciation or letting go of old thoughts before the new can find place in the consciousness. This is a psychological law, which has its outer expression in the intricate eliminative functions of the body."

"Letting go of old thoughts." What does Fillmore mean by that?

The term *old thoughts* means more than the thoughts on the conscious level of mind; it means those beliefs, attitudes, and automatic emotional responses that have been impressed in the subconscious level of mind and that dominate our behavior. Examples are: being oversensitive to criticism, impatience, a martyr-attitude, or a sense of inferiority. We could go on and on.

You know people of whom you have said, "I wish he (or she) would change his (or her) attitude." Well, what was this "attitude" you were referring to? It was a certain negative or inharmony-producing mental and emotional state in the person you were talking about. These negative states must go before the new attitudes and beliefs find a place.

The mind is just as real as the physical body. When there is a destructive virus or worn-out cells in your body, they have to be eliminated or they contaminate the body and cause illness.

Destructive emotional states, limited or fear beliefs, contaminate your mind just as a virus plays havoc in your body.

In fact, Fillmore suggests that because mind is cause and form is effect, disease germs may well be an effect caused by negative, God-empty thoughts and mental states such as greed, vanity, lust for power, guilt, pride and the rest.

Remember the song lyrics, "Accentuate the positive, eliminate the negative"? There is more truth than poetry there. It is not enough to "plaster on" positive thoughts—the old negative thoughts of guilt and greed, ambition and vanity fester underneath the veneer. The negative, as the song says, must be eliminated; this is where the faculty of renunciation comes in.

Denial is an expression of the faculty of renunciation or getting rid of, eliminating the negative.

To deny is to cleanse, clear out, release, make a vacuum for the positive to come in. A typical and effective denial is this:

> *I am free from tension, stress,*
> *and strain. I completely depend on*
> *infinite Wisdom to guide me*
> *into right action.*

Here, you are speaking the word of authority, first to deny and eliminate the mental/emotional states of tension, stress, and strain, then to affirm or build a new mental state—one of faith, trust, complete reliance and dependency on God.

When you have reason to use this denial and affirmation, I suggest that you focus your attention at the lower spine as you speak the denial, and then at the solar plexus, the physical center for wisdom, as you make the affirmation of dependency on infinite Wisdom:

> *I am free from tension, stress,*

and strain. I completely depend
on infinite Wisdom to guide me
into right action. I am grateful.

Now we come to the time when we quit
intellectualizing about the importance of the
faculty of renunciation and do something about
quickening, awakening, and spiritualizing that
remarkable and critical faculty of mind through
meditation.

Relax, make yourself comfortable. Lean back
into those everlasting arms in which you live,
move, and have your being.

Recall the passage in Paul's letter to the
Colossians: "The mystery hidden for ages and
generations but now made manifest . . . .
Christ in you, the hope of glory"
(Col. 1:26,27). Think to yourself:

The Christ of God indwells me.

Repeat it.

This is a mind-expanding idea that may be
difficult, at first, for your mind to accept.

Now let the focus of your attention move to
the crown of your head. This is the physical
center representing the Christ mind in you.
Affirm:

The Christ of God is
awakened in me.

Now bring your attention to your forehead.
Think of the forehead as representing the

conscious level of mind. Affirm:
> *I am consciously aware that*
> *the Christ of God is*
> *awakening in me.*

Next, move to the solar plexus. As you let
your attention dwell on this central part of
your body, which represents the subconscious
level of mind, affirm:
> *I am grateful that the Christ*
> *of God is awakening in me.*

Now let that spotlight of attention travel to
the end of your spine, the very lowest part of
your back. Affirm:
> *Christ in me quickens my faculty*
> *of renunciation. The activity*
> *of Spirit cleanses my mind of*
> *limited and false beliefs, making*
> *room for greater understanding*
> *and newness of life.*
> *I am grateful.*

The color that coordinates with the faculty
of renunciation is russet.

LIFE

Judas—Generative Center

Repetition being the mother of learning, let's review what we are doing and what has gone before.

Jesus, as we all know, had twelve disciples. Let us remember that these were not men who chose Jesus; rather, each was carefully and individually chosen by Jesus.

This is important to recognize, because it adds weight to the reasoning that Jesus had a special purpose in choosing these particular men.

Unity believes that Jesus' careful selection has to do with the fact that each disciple metaphysically symbolizes

A Twelve-Power Meditation Exercise

one of the twelve powers of mind through which the Christ in us expresses.

Charles Fillmore went further, to claim that each disciple-faculty also has a specific center in the physical body over which it rules.

Let me enumerate the disciples, the faculty of mind each represents, the location in the body, and the color that coordinates with that particular faculty:

DISCIPLE	FACULTY	LOCATION	COLOR
Peter	faith	Pineal gland	Deep blue
Andrew	strength	Small of back	Light green
James	wisdom	Solar plexus	Yellow
John	love	Behind the heart	Pink
Philip	power	Throat	Purple
Bartholomew	imagination	Between the eyes	Light blue
Thomas	understanding	Forehead	Gold
Matthew	will	Forehead	Silver
James, the son of Alphaeus	order	Navel	Deep green
Simon, the Zealot	zeal	Medulla oblongata, back of head	Orange
Thaddaeus	renunciation	Lower spine	Russet
Judas	life	Generative center	Red

Now to Judas, the last of the disciples, who represents the faculty of life. The area of the body governed by this faculty is the generative area of the lower abdomen.

78

Judas is the disciple who betrayed Jesus. Similarly, wrong, irresponsible, or wasteful use of the life principle by us betrays or stands in the way of the effortless unfolding of the Christ in us.

In many ways we misuse or waste the life energy that flows from the universal sea of life energy (God) through the individualized Christ in us.

Most of us have been tired, dragged out, exhausted, weary many times. This is seldom caused by actual physical labor, but rather by negative and destructive emotional states allowed to run riot.

Negative emotional states dissipate the flow of life energy and leave us weak and impotent.

For example: John Averageman reads the morning newspaper at breakfast and emotionally relates to all the negative news: the current political scandal, the dip in the stock market, accidents, bank robberies, and so on.

Then he goes off to work, fighting traffic, cursing as he chooses the wrong lane, and gets held up behind a stalled car; all the way to work his molars are grinding against each other.

At work there is an order cancellation and a memo from the boss that makes him tense and tingling with apprehension. At lunch he gets into an emotional discussion about inflation or politics or whatever.

He arrives home weary, and relaxes by spending the evening sipping martinis and dozing in front of the television. His wife complains that he isn't romantic anymore; she might as well be married to a zombie.

John Averageman has misused, or wastefully used, the all-important life faculty through emotional indulgence.

Visualize this same person going through a typical day without responding with a negative emotion to the innumerable temptations to do so.

He reads the morning paper objectively, without emotional judgment. He refuses to let traffic upset his calmness. He doesn't let the problems at work upset him, for he knows there will always be problems and in a month he won't even remember what today's problems were. Thus, with a serene mind he handles the problem creatively and successfully.

He arrives home relaxed, at peace, and just as in love with, appreciative of, and understanding toward his wife as in the first days of their marriage.

In short, negative attitudes and emotional states drain life energy and "betray" the indwelling Christ, which is trying to express and unfold through us.

The mental/emotional state of lust first comes to mind when one thinks of the life faculty and its center in the body. And lust, or continuous and excessive mental concentration on sex, and its inevitable emotional repercussions, will rob physical energy and keep us from operating at our best in every area of life. But lust isn't the only betrayer of life energy. Greed, ambition, vanity, and their lieutenant emotions of jealousy, hostility, impatience, resentment, self-pity, anger, and the long list of common but very unspiritual emotional states we sometimes entertain also deplete life energy.

Cora Fillmore, in her companion book to *The Twelve Powers of Man*, entitled *Christ Enthroned in Man*, states, "Judas represents the negative pole of life, located in the generative center, and Jesus the positive pole or spiritual center located in the crown of the head."

A flow of energy requires these two poles: positive and negative. But, if the negative pole is weakened, it automatically weakens the positive pole.

In short, if you weaken one, you weaken both. This means that when you weaken the life center through dissipating the life energy in emotional storms, you automatically weaken,

devitalize, and diminish the healing, reju-
venating life that flows from God, the source
of life.

Yes, the human body operates on much the
same principles that govern the power of
electricity. The cells are like little batteries, and
science has measured the charges of energy
they emit.

Strong emotions disrupt the power line.
They short-circuit the life energy, which burns
out cells, tissues, and organs. This we call
sickness. Then we childishly try to blame God
by crying out, "If God is supposed to be so
loving and good, why did this sickness come
upon me?"

This, you see, shifts the blame from our own
ego to God, even though in the next moment
we are appealing to God to heal us.

Let's complete this lesson with an example of
the type of prayer-affirmation you would make
to strengthen and spiritualize this all-important
faculty in you.

We would want to include the idea of mental
and emotional calmness and serenity, as well as
an acknowledgment of God as the source of all
life and of our own life.

Placing your center of attention at the lower
abdomen, speak these freeing, vitalizing words
of Truth:

The Christ in me is quickening my faculty of life, represented by the disciple Judas. I am calm, serene, and in complete mastery of my emotions, thus allowing the universal life-force to flow through me to heal, energize, and recharge my physical body. I am grateful.

The color that harmonizes with the life faculty is red.

A SUGGESTION

The complete Twelve-Power Meditation involves memorizing thirty-six items in a certain related order: twelve faculties, twelve corresponding disciples' names, and twelve body centers.

This is no easy task, and the temptation to give up may be strong. You may say to yourself, "I'm so busy intellectually trying to remember all the disciples, faculties, and body centers that I don't feel I am really meditating. I'm not really getting any good out of it."

To overcome this obstacle, work with the first four faculties only: faith (Peter); strength (Andrew); judgment (James, son of Zebedee); love (John); and their body centers. When you find you can speak the quickening words to these first four in proper order, work on the next four.

A Twelve-Power Meditation Exercise

The second four are all located in the head: power (Philip), throat; imagination (Bartholomew), between the eyes; understanding (Thomas) and will (Matthew), both located in the forehead.

Then the last four: order (James, son of Alphaeus), navel; zeal (Simon the Cananaean), back of neck; renunciation (Thaddaeus), lowest part of spine; life (Judas), generative area.

Like touch-typing, it may take an investment of time in the beginning, but when it infiltrates your subconscious and becomes automatic you will begin to experience the regenerating power of the Twelve-Power Meditation.

A Twelve-Power Meditation

The exercise as given here is a framework. You give it spiritual flesh and substance as you use affirmations that arise out of your own under-standing of the ideas represented by the twelve faculties of mind.

Place your attention at the crown of your head and say or think to yourself:

The Christ of God is
awakened in me.

The crown of the head represents the Christ center or superconscious level of mind.

Let the focal point of your attention move to the forehead with the thought:

A Twelve-Power Meditation Exercise

> *I am aware that the Christ*
> *of God is awakened in me.*

The forehead represents the conscious level of mind. That is why you use the words, *aware* or *I am conscious that.*

> *I am aware that the Christ*
> *of God is awakened in me.*

Let your focal point drop to the solar plexus region and affirm:

> *I am grateful that the Christ*
> *is awakened in me.*

(The solar plexus is the seat of the subconscious level of mind or the feeling level. Gratitude is primarily a feeling.)

Now, go to each of the disciple-centers in your body and let the Christ in you quicken that center. First, the disciple-faculty of faith, located in the middle of the head. In your own words convey the idea that:

> *Christ in me is quickening*
> *my faculty of faith.*

As you get used to the exercise you might add other thoughts such as:

> *The Christ in me is training*
> *my faculty of faith to detach*
> *itself from depending on outer*
> *conditions and helping it to*
> *focus on the presence and*
> *power of God.*

Then let your attention travel down to the small of the back, the office of the disciple-faculty of strength, Andrew. Affirm:
> *I am strong in the Lord.*
> *I am strength.*

After the faith center in the pineal gland, and the strength center at the small of the back, let your attention go to the solar plexus, the body-office of the faculty of wisdom, and affirm:
> *I am wisdom.*

James, the son of Zebedee, who represents wisdom, is the brother of John. John represents love, and is located just behind the heart. Jesus called these two brothers "sons of thunder." As you develop them spiritually, tremendous power is generated. Affirm at the love center:
> *I am love.*

Move your attention to the throat, which represents Philip, power. Affirm:
> *I am power.*

This will give power to the words you speak and a compelling resonance to your voice.

Now focus between your eyes, which is the physical center for Bartholomew, the faculty of imagination. Imagination is the "third eye" of creativity. Affirm:
> *My imagination is*
> *spiritually quickened.*

Move up a bit to the forehead, which is the

seat of both understanding and will. Thomas
represents understanding; Matthew represents
will.

Understanding is knowing that comes from
within. The will is the executive faculty. It
executes or carries out the orders of the Christ
and the other eleven faculties. Affirm:

> *The light of understanding*
> *enables me to see clearly.*
> *I take right action.*

From here, your attention goes to the center
behind the navel; James, the son of Alphaeus,
represents the faculty of order. Affirm:

> *My mind, body, and affairs*
> *are in divine order.*

Then move to the back of the neck: Simon,
called the Zealot or the Cananaean, represents
the power of zeal. Affirm:

> *I am filled with tireless energy*
> *to do what is mine to do.*

Next, move to the base of the spine;
Thaddaeus, the disciple-faculty of renunciation.
Affirm:

> *Christ in me is helping me to release*
> *and let go all that is limited, false,*
> *outworn, and that stands in the way*
> *of my spiritual unfoldment.*

Then, to the generative center ruled by
Judas, the disciple-faculty of life, affirm:

A Twelve-Power Meditation

The pure, restorative, cleansing
life of God is flowing through me
now. I feel it and I am grateful.

Close your meditation by again placing your attention at the Christ center at the crown of the head, and feel a soft, golden light flowing down over the length of your body. Then speak the "Prayer for Protection."

The light of God surrounds me;
The love of God enfolds me;
The power of God protects me;
The presence of God watches over me.
Wherever I am, God is!
I am grateful.

About the Author

Charles Roth was an ordained Unity minister and prolific writer for *Daily Word*® and *Unity Magazine*®. During his career, he served congregations in Des Moines, Iowa, and Detroit, Michigan. He also served as a member of the Unity Minister's Association executive board, as editor of the *Unity Minister's Journal,* as assistant to the editor of *Daily Word,* and as chairman of the Association of Unity Churches Educational Advisory Committee. He is the author of the book *Mind: The Master Power.*

Printed U.S.A.

B0102